Tea Party with Brielle

Written by
Brielle Vivienne & Jacqueline Regano

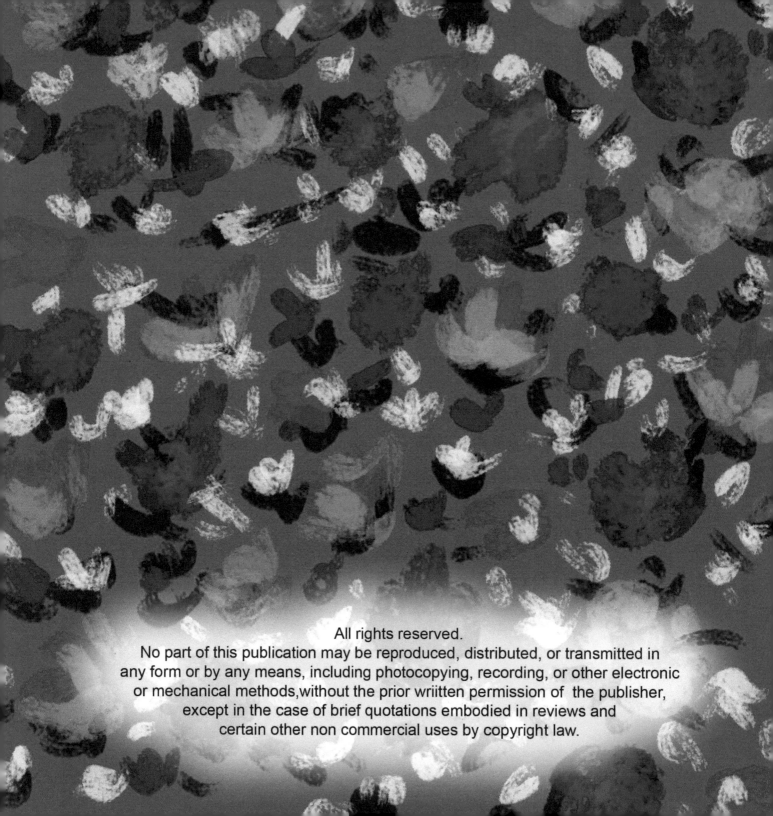

Brielle

Hosting a **tea party**
is **so much fun!**

First, I must
invite my guests!

Then,
pick a location.

If it is warm outside, I can set it up in the backyard. If it is chilly, I can ask my mommy to help me set up my tea party in my bedroom.

I need a table and enough
chairs for my guests.

My favorite part is picking out
a **theme** for my tea party!

Yes, there can be all kinds of themes!

It can be based on a color, a season,
an animal, or even a favorite cartoon character!

The theme I will choose for today will be floral!
A floral afternoon tea party!
Marvelous!

Now, I need to pick out
the most perfect outfit!
For a floral tea party, I will choose a floral dress!
Then, I put on my matching sparkly gold shoes
and, of course, a matching tea party headband!

I always **dress the table up!**

I love to put a pretty tablecloth and a runner!
I have all different colors.

For today, I will choose
a pink tablecloth
and a sparkly
gold runner!

Then, I get matching plates,
utensils, and napkins.

How pretty!

I put my teacups next to each guest's plate.
I put the tea kettle in the middle, and
I decorate the table with matching pink flowers.
Voila!
The table looks beautiful!

I must prepare the food for the table.
I love to include mini croissants and tea sandwiches.

Below are two recipes I like to make
and serve to my guests.

I always make sure the prepared food
is on a pretty plate or serving platter.

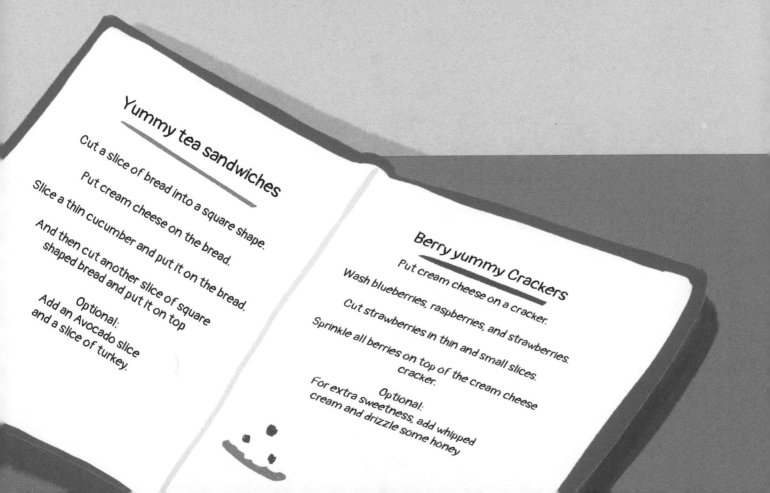

Yummy tea sandwiches

Cut a slice of bread into a square shape.

Put cream cheese on the bread.

Slice a thin cucumber and put it on the bread.

And then cut another slice of square shaped bread and put it on top

Optional:
Add an Avocado slice
and a slice of turkey.

Berry yummy Crackers

Put cream cheese on a cracker.

Wash blueberries, raspberries, and strawberries.

Cut strawberries in thin and small slices.

Sprinkle all berries on top of the cream cheese cracker.

Optional:
For extra sweetness, add whipped cream and drizzle some honey

Finally, I make my tea.

Today, I will make my yummy
chamomile-honey-berry-delish tea!

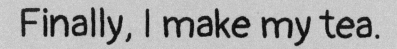

Tea recipe

(1 chamomile tea bag,
1tsp of honey,
a few blueberries,
raspberries
and cut up strawberries)

HONEY

My guests will be arriving soon.

I will now make sure I have all the right
accessories for my floral afternoon tea party!

I take out extra flower hats and headbands,
flower crowns, and some pretty capes.

Magic wands are a must!
We can play with all the accessories!

My guests have finally arrived!
I am going to go host now.

See you at my
next party!

Bye!

Follow Brielle on Instagram
@briellevivienne